# This Is My Library

**Adam Bellamy**

**Enslow Publishing**
101 W. 23rd Street
Suite 240
New York, NY 10011
USA

enslow.com

Published in 2017 by Enslow Publishing, LLC.
101 W. 23rd Street, Suite 240, New York, NY 10011

**Library of Congress Cataloguing-in-Publication Data**
Names: Bellamy, Adam.
Title: This is my library / Adam Bellamy.
Description: New York : Enslow Publishing, 2017 | Series: All about my world | Includes bibliographical references and index.
Identifiers:  ISBN 9780766080898 (pbk.) | ISBN 9780766080928 (library bound) | ISBN 9780766080911 (6 pack)
Subjects: LCSH: Libraries--Juvenile literature.
Classification: LCC Z665.5 B45 2017 | DDC 027--dc23

Printed in China

**To Our Readers:** We have done our best to make sure all websites in this book were active and appropriate when we went to press. However, the author and the publisher have no control over and assume no liability for the material available on those websites or on any websites they may link to. Any comments or suggestions can be sent by e-mail to customerservice@enslow.com.

**Photo Credits:** Cover, p. 1 wavebreakmedia/Shutterstock.com; peiyang/Shutterstock.com (globe icon on spine); pp. 3 (left), 20 Blend Images/Shutterstock.com; pp. 3 (center), 18 Tyler Olson/Shutterstock.com; pp. 3 (right), 14 parinyabinsuk/Shutterstock.com; p. 4–5 Melinda Fawver/Shutterstock.com; p. 6 Phil McDonald/Shutterstock.com; p. 8 Karl Gehring/Denver Post/Getty Images; p. 10 Celig/Shutterstock.com; p. 12 Andresr/Shutterstock.com; p. 16 © AP Images; p. 22 Sergey Novikov/Shutterstock.com.

# Contents

# Words to Know

check out     librarian     library card

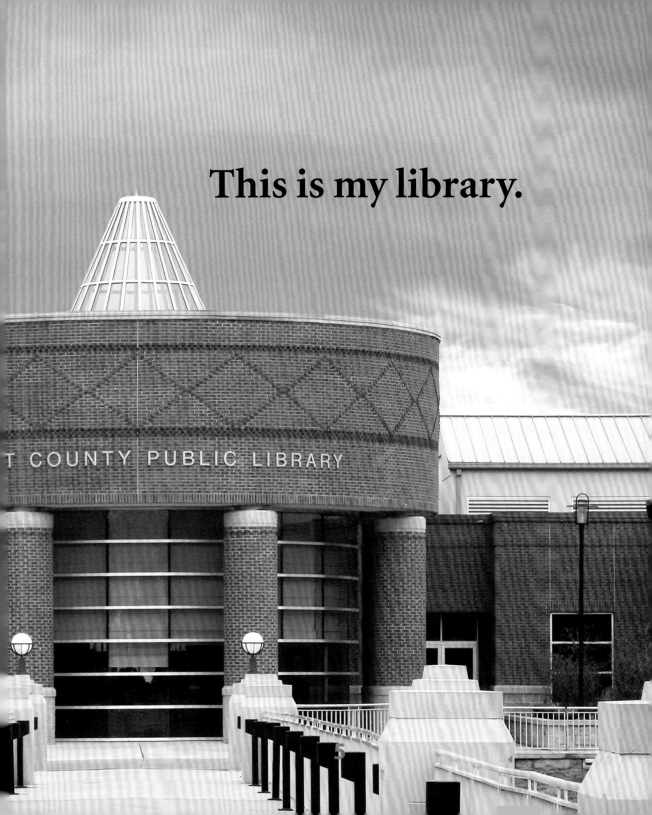

This is my library.

The library has thousands of books, magazines, and newspapers. It has movies, too!

Some libraries are big. Others are small. Some libraries are even on wheels!

I use a library card to borrow books. When I am finished reading them, I bring the books back.

The library also has computers that anyone can use.

You have to be quiet in a library. Many people are reading.

But there are other fun things at libraries, too. There are games, story time, and sometimes book sales.

The librarian keeps the books neat and helps people find the books they need.

The librarian also helps me check out books so I can take them home.

Going to the library is fun!

# Read More

Bellisario, Gina. *Let's Meet a Librarian.* Minneapolis, MN: Millbrook Press, 2013.

Rissman, Rebecca. *Going to a Library.* Mankato, MN: Heinemann-Raintree, 2012.

Rosenstock, Barb. *Thomas Jefferson Builds a Library.* Honesdale, PA: Calkins Creek Books, 2013.

# Websites

**Association for Library Service to Children**
*www.ala.org/alsc/kickstart*
A list of activities and programs for kids at libraries across the US.

**Library of Congress**
*www.loc.gov/visit/activities-for-kids-and-families*
Fun things to do at the Library of Congress in Washington, DC.

# Index

Guided Reading Level: B
Guided Reading Leveling System is based on the guidelines recommended by Fountas and Pinnell.

Word Count: 122